BUSTER BOOKS

COLOURMETRICS

DESIGNED BY
JACK CLUCAS

EDITED BY
EMMA TAYLOR

COVER DESIGN BY
ANGIE ALLISON

Complete the twenty-one pictures in this book using the
vibrant and striking colour palettes on each page. Simply
follow the number codes that accompany each image.

Don't worry if you don't have pens or pencils that exactly
match the colours shown. Get creative – darker colours can be
achieved by applying more pressure with a pencil, and lighter
hues by pressing gently. You could even produce new colours by
blending two shades together. On some of the pages you will notice
blank shapes without numbers inside. These should be left white.

There are finished versions of the pictures at the back of the
book, just in case you can't wait to find out what they look like.

With images adapted from www.shutterstock.com

First published in Great Britain in 2021 by Buster Books, an imprint of
Michael O'Mara Books Limited, 9 Lion Yard, Tremadoc Road, London SW4 7NQ

 www.mombooks.com/buster   Buster Books   @BusterBooks   @buster_books

A CIP catalogue record for this book is available from the British Library.

ISBN: 978-1-78055-748-9

3 5 7 9 10 8 6 4 2

This book was printed in May 2023 by
Shenzhen Wing King Tong Paper Products Co. Ltd.,
Shenzhen, Guangdong, China.